SUMMARY

&ANALYSIS

OF

Being Mortal

Medicine and What Matters in the End

A GUIDE TO THE BOOK
BY ATUL GAWANDE

NOTE: This book is a summary and analysis and is meant as a companion to, not a replacement for, the original book.

Please follow this link to purchase a copy of the original book: https://amzn.to/2laF7gh

TABLE OF CONTENTS

SYNOPSIS

Being Mortal is author Atul Gawande's commentary on modern approaches to aging and death. Gawande focuses his commentary primarily on Western treatment of death and dying, going as deep as its philosophical and attitudinal roots. He offers candid, though compassionate, criticism of the current state of affairs with end-of-life issues, proposing an alternate approach that is foreign but simple.

Gawande says that the Western approach to death is largely medical. In many ways, people refuse to accept that they will die, viewing death as a sickness to be treated rather than an unflinching reality. He supplies numerous anecdotes of terminally ill individuals using any and every method to stave off death: medicine with debilitating side-effects, invasive surgery, and exhausting, largely-futile therapy. Gawande questions if more time, regardless of quality, is really the best thing for the dying.

The book's core is a simple question: what if life could be better for the dying? It may be the case that we really don't know what we want out of life, or more importantly, out of death. Through his stories and wealth of experience in the medical field, Gawande argues that the ends of our lives can be far better than they are now, and it all starts with accepting that death is inevitable in one way or another, and it is in many ways better to work with death than against it.

KEY TAKEAWAYS & ANALYSIS

Key Takeaway: The Western approach to end-of-life care is primarily medical in nature.

This takeaway is the hinge of just about everything Gawande talks about in the book. Most people treat death and aging as medical conditions that can be cured or treated, rather than an uncomfortable inevitability. Gawande points out the fact that many people die in a hospital attempting to "get better," a practice that in all prior human history would seem as puzzling as it is strange. More than any other time in history, thanks to advances in the medical field, people are willing to undergo any number of treatments, trials, and procedures and will pay the exorbitant bills that accompany them, all for the remote chance of staving off death for a few months or years.

Gawande notes that death is somewhat of a medical mystery, though a few schools of thought on aging have gained prominence. Some scholars believe that death is a genetically-orchestrated event, a process that begins at a predestined time for adaptive reasons. This is evidenced by the vastly different lifespans of similar species with similar physical burdens, e.g. the emperor goose (6.3 years on average) as compared to the Canada goose (23.5 years on average). It seems, though, that the more convincing theory is that aging and death are the result of accumulating wear-and-tear. Years of exposure to the elements, injuries, sickness, and natural aging effects make the body more fragile, unable to fully recover from sickness and decay. At some point, the body cannot perform its vital functions and either succumbs to illness or ceases to function. It appears that a majority of professionals subscribe to the wear-and-tear model.

The wear-and-tear theory lends itself to a medical approach to aging, so many, if not most, doctors are trained to see death as a syndrome, focusing on the symptoms and complications that naturally precede death. Hence, the dominant attitude in Western medicine is that the primary role of the physician is to cure sickness and extend life as long as the patient permits. This is an unsurprising phenomenon, notes Gawande, with the rapid and tremendous advances in medical science over the past century or so. There is no disease at this point in history that cannot at least be managed with surgery or medicine. There is never an excuse to do nothing; patients always have the ability to ask, "what's next?" when something goes wrong or does not work.

Whereas decline in the past was precipitous and sudden, death has now become gradual and slow. Death used to represent a near-instantaneous dive from ability to mortality. Now, death is an accumulation of disabilities. Myriad devices and therapies have created a new middle-ground between old age and death, a middle-ground of successive loss until one is totally incapacitated, if one chooses to prolong their death so far. The old model of care was acceptance and preparation. Now, the model is self-preservation. Gawande does not necessarily oppose the extension of life. However, he does not believe that the medical model sufficiently cares for the whole person during this gradual decline it has created.

Gawande, whose family immigrated to America from India, notes that many factors play into a society's general approach to death. Culture is one such factor. In developing countries, for example, it is normal for aging persons, upon losing the capacity to live alone, to move in with their children to be cared for by them. This practice is completely foreign to much of the modern West, as its core individualism does not so readily allow such a burden to descend on a person or family; hence, Western families often opt for medical treatment or senior residential services rather than caring for their elders themselves. Wealth also factors in. The reality is that many of the riskier, more aggressive interventions in aging and dying are quite expensive and are only available to those people with the requisite wealth. Development is equally important in end-of-life care. Underdeveloped cultures may not have the physicians or technology to more aggressively fight off death. These cultures may opt for palliative care out of necessity rather than preference.

Certain philosophical values underlie a society's treatment of aging and death as well. The West is defined by its individualism, its undying emphasis on the person, his or her freedom, and the rights of the individual over the community. In general, people will fight to regain more independence rather than settle for less, driving them to endure risky procedures and treatment to maximize independence. Gawande writes, "Our reverence for independence takes no account of the reality of what happens in life: sooner or later, independence will become impossible" (p. 22). Ironically, people will surrender independence now, in the case of serious illness like cancer, to gain more independence later. People want to give their individualism as long a time horizon as possible. As mentioned above, the same attitude applies to senior care, as families will opt for a third-party organization to care for aging loved ones rather than taking the burden on themselves.

The medical model does not manifest only in the final few days of a person's life but rather throughout the whole span of age-related decline. Many of our gerontological services adopt a medical, "safe" approach when it comes to care for the elderly. Nursing homes, one of the most ubiquitous residential options for the elderly, were created to solve overcrowding in hospitals by people who were too sick to live alone but not sick enough to warrant a room in the hospital. From their medical origins came an emphasis on sanitation, safety, and physical wellness above all else. Elderly residents of nursing homes or similar medical facilities often end up in these places due to loss of physical or cognitive function, and their independence is further diminished in order to push off further decline. People losing their balance may be relegated to a wheelchair permanently, even if walking is still possible. Others may be given a strictly pureed diet to avoid choking. These residents undergo a lengthy regimen of medication. They remain in bed for extended periods for rest and treatment. In all, their environment is designed to circumvent the risks of age-related fragility.

Key Takeaway: The medical model is flawed.

Gawande does not find the medical approach to aging particularly appealing. However, he does not deny that it is well-intentioned and that it does offer certain benefits. The medical model seeks to alleviate the worst parts of aging: choking, falling, cancer, isolation, etc. Frankly, the Western world is fairly good at the medical model, and medical professionals are only learning how to better overcome and resist the decay of aging. The medical model also provides hope for the hopeless, and there are cases, rare cases, of people overcoming apparent death, such as a miraculous recovery from stage-four cancer, earning another decade with loved ones. No matter how remote the chance, the medical model provides hope that something can turn for the better—a chance that is eliminated when palliative measures (to be described below) are adopted.

Many things make the medical model appealing to organizations and residences, but certainly not the least of them is cost-effectiveness. A medical approach often requires fewer staff and fewer variable costs than its counterpart. The medical model is also efficient; it is far easier to create one-size-fits-all routines, programs, and treatment than it is to adapt to each individual's particular needs. Cash-strapped organizations may resort to a medical model out of necessity. Staffing and paying for special outings, adjusting routines to each individual, and running lower-census homes at times become a matter of the haves and the have-nots.

That said, the medical model is fraught with problems, says Gawande, problems that indeed increase longevity, but at a steep price. In short, it is grasping at an unrealistic hope of a good life later at the expense of quality life now.

Though the medical model is quite effective at extending life, it cannot put off death forever. The patients of that medical care, though, tend to focus more on the unrealistic hope of a few more years rather than confronting the reality of their mortality. The medical model perpetuates the fountain of youth myth: the belief that there's always a chance at full recovery, perhaps with the help of some risky surgery that may leave them in excruciating pain, or perhaps after a trial with an experimental drug with debilitating side-effects. This hope, which rarely considers the cold, hard facts and figures of terminal illness, clouds patients' judgment, convincing them to choose a life that they would never want to live.

Further complicating the decisions that patients must make is the unfair expectations that the medical model places on patients. People are sometimes so convinced of the efficacy of medical services that doing anything but the most aggressive, risky treatment appears cowardly or selfish, leading to hurt feelings, the perception that one is giving up, or that one is simply stupid. Indeed, there is such a nobility in being "a fighter," but it is widely expected that people go to heroic lengths to be one, as though fighting against the dying of the light was the *summum bonum*.

Ironically, research has in many instances found that aggressive medical interventions in terminal illness, such as chemotherapy, actually shorten the amount of time a person has left. Gambling is inherent in the medical model, as there is an element in uncertainty regarding how one's body will respond to treatment.

The tension between the medical model and other models of care boils down to two opposing values: longevity and quality of life. Is it better to endure discomfort, at times extreme discomfort, for the chance of recovery later? Can you weigh the decision in numbers and years?

The worst of this tension can be seen in facilities such as certain deplorable nursing homes. Gawande recounts nightmarish stories of once-vibrant individuals losing their luster after a fall or medical emergency scares family members into shoving them into some impersonal senior facility with gruel-like meals, infantile activities, and a clinical atmosphere. In these instances, a home is replaced with a hospital and life with a treatment plan. In these settings, people are often denied the things that made life so meaningful, such as the ability to eat a piece of pizza or the freedom to take a walk around the block, all in the name of avoiding risk.

The fact is that the medical model has no concern for the soul. The medical model is an empirical method that identifies problems and treats them. It presupposes that the person will find their own fulfillment elsewhere apart from the treatment. However, we never get to practice death.

Death is the ultimate unknown. We often don't know how to cope with death, but rather than help people deal with this realization, the medical model implicitly communicates that death is awful and must be avoided at all costs. This is a subtle point. The medical model doesn't so much affirm life as it condemns death. The medical model isn't expected to show people the meaning of life, but it should not impede choices that affirm a life-meaning that doesn't involve pervasive medical interventions. Unfortunately, this model often does, as it is a mindset that does not understand, nor is concerned with, the meaning of life.

Surely, it's never as easy as "this or that." There are gradations in our medical interventions; for example, many degrees separate antibiotics and a ventilator, as well as the quality of life associated with each treatment. It is up to the patient, under the guidance of his or her medical professional, to find their desired ratio between sacrifice and potential gain. Nevertheless, given the choice, people seem more willing to part with the quality of their life than their time. Why? Again, people don't want to come face-to-face with death. It's the great uncertainty, and it's scary to many.

Key Takeaway: A life worth living involves not just time, but the ability to make meaningful choices, which always carry risks.

The medical approach to end-of-life issues often makes erroneous assumptions about what a good life looks like. Or rather, as Gawande writes:

"The problem with medicine and the institutions it has spawned for the care of the sick and the old is not that they have had an incorrect view of what makes life significant. The problem is they have had almost no view at all. Medicine's focus is narrow. Medical professionals concentrate on repair of health, not sustenance of the soul" (p. 126)

It is assumed that a good life is pain-free and safe. When people think about it, though, they would much rather have the things they love in their lives and take the risk of having them than being safe without them. Gawande shares, sometimes amusingly, that people in nursing homes may sneak in chips or other choking hazards when they are on a choke-free diet. Others sneak in booze even though it may cause them to fall or may react with their medications. Still others may refuse to take certain medications because the pills make them feel sick or dizzy.

The point is that many times people wrongly assume that time is inherently valuable. The medical approach to aging suggests that more time means more happiness, or that it is better to fight for more time than make the most of what remains. But there isn't a direct correlation between time alive and happiness. Happiness comes from pursuing our interests and living out our values with people we love.

Gawande mentions a study that surveyed the behaviors of people who were near to death and those who weren't. Those who felt as though they had a lot of life ahead of them expressed desires to meet people who inspired them or could help advance them in their careers, to try new experiences, and to focus on their careers. People who were closer to death, on the other hand, preferred to spend time on hobbies, on calling and spending time with friends and family, and enjoying favorite foods and activities. People's priorities change when they confront death rather than ignore it. It's understandable that people in the West tend towards a medical approach to death and aging because they envision themselves having a longer time-horizon than they may realistically have. Is it realistic for a person with metastatic cancer to anticipate another five years to live? Were they to confront the inevitability of their death, Gawande suggests, they may opt for palliative care so they could have more moments of connection with their families or time to do the things they love.

People who find meaning in their daily lives appear to enjoy a greater sense of overall well-being. People want to give their lives meaning and often pursue causes greater than themselves, such as religion, politics, or justice. These transcendental meanings may even supersede traditional hierarchies of human needs, such as that famously put forward by Abraham Maslow. For some people, meaningful causes rise above even the peak of his pyramid, self-actualization, or at the very least, the two are bound up in one another.

To this point, Gawande points to an aging facility that had gone stale and become too clinical in the opinion of the medical director. He saw a preponderance of depression among his elderly patients, and he wanted to infuse life into the place. He decided, despite hesitation from the facility director, to have hundreds of parakeets delivered to the facility for the residents to keep and care for as pets. There was an immediate and remarkable uptick in well-being. Gawande suggests that the residents, who before either participated in meaningless activities or isolated themselves doing nothing, were invigorated by their newfound usefulness and purpose. People will devote themselves to many things, even the care of birds, especially when they have felt their lives devoid of meaning for a time.

People crave a purpose in their lives; we don't want time for the sake of time, but rather we want time to accomplish the things that matter to us. Medical professionals and gerontologists must consider this when making decisions about the health and wellness of their patients. Is a medicated, boring, though safe existence in the best interest of an aging or dying person? This lesson is especially pertinent to aging services, services that tend to prioritize safety over independence.

Of course, this is not always the case; many senior services are learning to balance safety and adaption with meaning and independence. Gawande describes numerous organizations that seek a less-restrictive approach to senior care. Many senior communities and residences propose safety measures without imposing them. Residents with declining abilities to swallow may have the choice to eat pizza, even if it presents the risk of choking or aspiration. Rather than take away the freedom to eat the pizza, some organizations are providing safety measures in the case that something goes wrong, such as call buttons for staff, granting their patients and residents the dignity of risk. Other facilities make efforts to meet residents where they are, trying to figure out what is important to them and working to incorporate those things into the day-to-day.

What the medical model misses is that the hardest part about death is often not death itself. Dying people often come up against tremendous depression, anxiety, and frustration when confronted with the progressive loss associated with death. The loss of choices makes life uninteresting and divests people from life. The loss of ability makes it harder to do the things one loved. Of course, people may be willing to sacrifice liberties for life, but there needs to be a line drawn with the patient's guidance.

Key Takeaway: Palliative care might be the best approach to death.

In this book, Gawande often contrasts the medical model with the palliative care model. Palliative care is an approach to dying that aims to reduce suffering and facilitate the dying process. Palliative care is often called dying with dignity because it eschews the uglier elements of the medical model, such as NG tubes, ventilators, and ileostomies, among other things. Those who choose palliative care are not holding out hope for a miraculous recovery, and they don't even hope to get more time; rather, they desire to go peacefully. They accept death in order to enjoy the time remaining, to focus on tying up loose ends and sending off their loved ones fondly.

The medical model isn't perfect, to be sure, but it seems depressing to simply throw one's hands up and wait for death. It is imperative that the decision between treatment and palliative care be made by the patient. It is the responsibility of the physician, says Gawande, to inform the patient of the different options and their pros and cons, and where appropriate, the doctor should try to provide guidance towards the more desirable option. However, the doctor must understand what the patient wants before providing guidance. If a person would rather fight now and try for the recovery, then that is their choice.

That said, patients often don't understand exactly what they want when in the proximity of death and all the stress that entails. When people opt for aggressive treatment and the medical model, it is often because they envision years ahead of time with loved ones and time to do the things they love. What they do not always acknowledge is the far more likely reality that these days never come and are replaced with months of tubes, therapy, pain, and debilitation. Even when the odds are drastically in favor of a continued decline, people are optimists, as Gawande says. People want to believe that they are special, that they are the exception, that they will work harder, endure more pain, and want recovery more than anyone else, even when these things are only part of the equation.

Of course, there can be a happy medium. Some people would gladly give up use of their legs in a risky spinal surgery if it provides a chance at being cancer-free or if it at least gives them a reasonable shot at another five years. Others would surely move into a slightly more restrictive home with greater supervision if it meant they wouldn't have to worry so much about falling. Some people just want to be able to eat ice cream and watch football, as Gawande recounts in one anecdote, and they will let that principle determine their risk-tolerance. There is no one-size-fit-all option for people facing death; there needs to be choice.

Nevertheless, it should be acknowledged that the thing people hope for in the future can often be had now, and all without the suffering that comes with aggressive, heroic efforts to delay death, in the case of terminal illness, or the beige mediocrity of life in a clinicalized senior facility, in the case of aging. Palliative care won't necessarily give people more life, but it will ensure that there is more life in the time they have left.

There is an unfortunate consequence to holding too strictly to the medical model: the last memories of the dying person are often sad. Constant suffering. Feeding tubes. Minimal consciousness. Heartbreaking setbacks. Rather than a miraculous recovery, people often watch their loved ones go through a fate worse than death. The medical model assumes that death is the ultimate failure, something to be avoided at all costs. However, it is difficult to imagine death being worse than the side-effects of aggressive treatments, progressive organ failure, and delirious minds under a cloud of pain and medication.

Strangely enough, Gawande notes that research suggests palliative care might actually be better at lengthening lives than aggressive medical intervention. Part of this can be explained by the fact that the range of time gained from medical interventions is much larger than palliative care. Although some people who undergo chemotherapy might gain a few years, most patients end up wearing their bodies down faster, making them more vulnerable to fatal infection or diseases. Palliative care, on the other hand, seeks to maintain and address symptoms of discomfort without wearing the body out. Unsurprisingly, palliative care can also reduce stress and improve outlook on life, as it removes many of the stresses that come with battling fatal disease.

Ultimately, Gawande suggests that physicians do more than focus on curing disease; he thinks doctors should help people have the best of their lives. To be clear, he doesn't oppose attempting to cure diseases. Rather, he warns against doctors having tunnel-vision, just as he warns families from focusing too much on their loved one's physical health when making decisions about senior care. Doctors are trained to determine the options, present the pros and cons of each, and help guide patients to the best option, all of which are good and useful services. However, Gawande says that the first things doctors should do is help patients figure out what they want. Not every patient wants to stretch their lives to the furthest possible horizon.

Gawande doesn't fault doctors for trying to guide patients. Navigating a medical emergency is a complicated situation for someone without years of study and experience in the medical field. It's understandable why a doctor would take the reins and try to steer a patient toward what makes the most sense medically. Patients will probably default to whatever the doctor says, which makes life easier for the physician, but obviously that doesn't guarantee that his or her real needs are being met. For this reason, a doctor needs to involve the patient by understanding the patient and his or her wishes.

Part of this entails being realistic with patients. It is not that doctors are dishonest. Rather, studies show that patients and doctors have expectations that don't fit with statistics. Patients and physicians are often overly optimistic, which makes deciding on the best course of action difficult. There is a big difference between a potential five year gain and a year at best, though more likely a few months, when deciding on chemotherapy. It is often the case that doctors don't want to come off as being harsh or seeming like they aren't willing to help, which is understandable. After all, unlikely recoveries are impossible when an attempt isn't made. However, false hope does no favors for patients. In fact, as noted above, unnecessary aggression in treating terminal illnesses often shortens lives rather than lengthens them when compared to palliative care. Doctors need to give honest assessments and provide reasonable hope. Doctors also need to be honest about the costs of aggressive treatments and fighting to the end. Patients need to see that there is also value in dying with dignity, reducing suffering, being conscious to best enjoy what time is left with the people and things that made them want to live longer in the first place.

Ultimately, a happy life is one rich with meaning. People find meaning in different ways, whether through religion, caring for others, working towards a goal, or spending time with loved ones.

EDITORIAL REVIEW

Atul Gawande's *Being Mortal* is a timely book. Issues of death and dying are making headlines and sparking debate in the West, and people are starting to grasp how much choice nowadays goes into dying. Do I go gently into the good night or rage against it? Am I willing to go on life support? Gawande delves into these issues that people face to expose the errors we as a country make when looking death in the face, and he suggests a better way in the process.

The book itself is largely anecdotal, though he successfully ties the stories back to his theories. The ideas and issues at hand are always tied to real people to whom we can relate, and Gawande doesn't hide the complexity of the questions we face. These aren't straw-men arguments of lifeless senior homes and foolish ventures onto life-support. There is no denial of the grades of grey in these questions, nor is there a suggestion that one size fits all. At times, the book could benefit from some paring down of the stories, but Gawande successfully captures the drama of the human experience while connecting it to the broader questions at hand.

This book is approachable, but Gawande still carries a tone of authority throughout. This is emphasized by the fact that Gawande shares some of his personal experiences, including experiences with his father's aging. It is clear that he knows what he is talking about, but at no point does one sniff jargon or pomposity. This is a book that readers of all levels can pick up and learn from. There was surely a temptation to delve into philosophy and make this book into a tome, but

Gawande does well to keep the book lively without sacrificing substance.

Gawande's thesis is pretty convincing and he provides plenty of reasoning and evidence for his claims. He balances his anecdotes with data and incorporates nuance where it is appropriate, so it is difficult to disagree with him. Many of the suggestions in the book will be met with confusion or frustration, such as allowing choke-risk patients to eat whatever they want, but this is to be expected since the medical model is the status quo.

If there is one criticism of the book, it's that it drags a bit in the middle as Gawande talks about Western senior services. He may have been better served to pare down some of his stories, perhaps merging a couple of chapters and giving a broader look at these things. However, it is informative nonetheless, and the book picks up on the back end.

Overall, Gawande has provided an insightful look into a topic that is both uncomfortable and beautiful. For a book about death, *Being Mortal* teaches a lot about life, that we shouldn't measure life chronologically but experientially. Its appeal is universal and is a worthy read for casual and serious readers alike.

BACKGROUND ON AUTHOR

Atul Gawande, M.D., M.P.H. is a writer, researcher and surgeon in Boston, MA. Gawande writes about his experiences in the medical field and currently conducts research to increase innovation in healthcare.

Gawande has written four *New York Times* Bestsellers, and he has been a writer for *The New Yorker* since 1998. He has twice won a National Magazine Award for his contributions as a journalist.

Gawande continues to practice surgery in Boston at Brigham and Women's Hospital. He operates in general and endocrine surgery there.

The MacArthur Fellows Program awarded Gawande a fellowship for his writing on medicine and its practice in developed nations. He also received a fellowship from the Hastings Center.

In 2007, Gawande was named the head of the World Health Organization's effort to reduce surgical mortality rates.

OTHER TITLES BY ATUL GAWANDE:

Complications: A Surgeon's Note on an Imperfect Science (2002)

Better: A Surgeon's Note on Performance (2007)

The Checklist Manifesto: How to Get Things Right (2009)

*** END OF BOOK SUMMARY***

*If you enjoyed this **ZIP Reads** publication, we encourage you to purchase a copy of the original book.*

We'd also love an honest review on Amazon.com!

56713547R00015

Made in the USA
Columbia, SC
30 April 2019